TABLE
CHIC

Dedication

To my husband Ed, my daughter Natasha and my stepdaughters Sienna and Savannah, who have provided me with great inspiration to create this book

TABLE
CHIC

KELLY HOPPEN

text by KATHY PHILLIPS

LAUREL
GLEN

Published in the United States by
Laurel Glen Publishing
5880 Oberlin Avenue, Suite 400
San Diego, CA 92121-4794
http://www.advantagebooksonline.com

Published in Great Britain in 1997 by Collins & Brown Limited
London House, Great Eastern Wharf, Parkgate Road, London SW11 4NQ

Library of Congress Cataloging-in-Publication Data

Hoppen, Kelly.
    Table chic / Kelly Hoppen : text by Kathy Phillips.
        p.   cm.
    "First published in Great Britain in 1997 by Collins & Brown.
Limited"--T.p. verso.
    ISBN 1-57145-651-1
    1. Table setting and decoration. I. Phillips, Kathy. II. Title.
TX879.H67 1997
642'.7--dc21   97-30240
                                                                    CIP

2 3 4 5 97 98 99 01

Conceived, edited and designed by Collins & Brown Limited

Editor: Gillian Haslam
Designer: Christine Wood
Photography: Andreas von Einsiedel
Stylist: Arabella McNie

Reproduction by Daylight Colour Art
Printed and bound in Hong Kong by Sino Publishing House Ltd

$\mathcal{C}$ONTENTS

FOREWORD *by Lucia van der Post*

*I*F EVER ANYBODY doubted that taking trouble over setting a table was worth the effort, this book should cure them forever. Here is a visual paeon to the seductive powers of the imaginatively dressed table. Nobody who was lucky enough to be invited to join a gathering round one of Kelly Hoppen's endlessly imaginative settings could fail to sense the spirits lift. Here are joyous tables, tables that celebrate the perennial delights of food, of family, of friendship, of love. They are also a tribute to the power of the aesthetic eye and the inventive spirit. Here are ideas that are accessible to all. Very often no great sums of money are involved – with a few carefully chosen flowers, candles and the simple tableware that is to be found in almost everybody's kitchen, the dining table can become a source of daily delight. The family meal, the grand dinner, the evening *à deux*, the country breakfast, can be turned into celebratory events that soothe the soul and linger in the memory. The very same table can be lushly sensuous one evening, coolly modernist the next. It can be prettily rustic or calmingly oriental, crisply welcoming or overflowing with baroque splendour. When such magic can be conjured out of such simple props it seems a pity not to read the book and heed its message – with a little trouble, a careful eye and Kelly Hoppen's inspirational settings to guide us, even the most routine of meals need never be dull again.

INTRODUCTION

*A*S AN INTERIOR DESIGNER, an important part of my job is to find new ways of being creative, and I have increasingly found myself applying this instinct to the table. Planning a table setting for a particular occasion can be such fun – deciding on the theme, selecting linen and china, and choosing the flowers.

I love entertaining but, between the pressures of family and work, I don't really have the time to enjoy the process of cooking a meal and I believe the spirit of a gathering is influenced far more by the company you are in and the surroundings – important though the food is. A few years ago, friends and design clients began asking me to help with tables for special occasions and I realized I found the process of creating not only the table but the mood for the party very rewarding. The aim of this book is therefore not simply to be a guidebook to be slavishly copied, but also to stimulate your own imagination. You will undoubtedly find inspiration for a whole host of your own ideas simply by looking at the photographs that follow.

I have included a number of my special tricks, including the creative use of runners and ribbon, proving that a chic table does not have to be expensive. The style comes from the creative blending of ideas and materials. I hope that you will enjoy the book and will be inspired to create your own style of *Table Chic*.

Kelly Hoppen

$\mathcal{C}$OLOR

*T*HE WAY YOU USE COLOR in a table setting is of paramount importance. It can provide either the starting point for the whole theme or just an accent that sings out from a display of neutral tones — a splash of brilliance in the form of flowers, napkins, plates, glasses or ribbons.

It can be used to echo a color that is already part of the room's decoration, or to set a mood. Think pink for a little girl's christening buffet, for instance; green for a table set in the garden; red, silver and gold as traditional Christmas shades; or a riot of bright colors all jostling together, to make a cheerful, party atmosphere.

Two strongly contrasting colors can provide the basis for a very stylish table setting. Here, black and white provide an ideal background for a dramatic sixties' themed table. The deep-red flowers and green leaves of two vases of tulips add vibrant splashes of color which have all the more impact through being used in only two, symmetrically positioned vases.

On the glass and chrome table, which was the starting point for the whole scheme, I laid out randomly a collection of black and white rectangular plates. A square black bowl might top a rectangular white plate at one place setting, with a large black rectangular plate under a smaller white one next to it.

In the middle of the table, rather than a conventional candelabra or floral display, I opted for neat white storage jars because their

RIGHT: *Playing with positive and negative, the simple combination of black and white provides a dramatic background for this elegant dinner party.*

BLACK AND WHITE SIXTIES' STYLE

strong lines echo the table's theme. They could, of course, be functional as well as decorative and could be used to hold sugar, mints, or cookies to serve with coffee at the end of the meal.

The rectangles and squares make the whole setting look quite geometric, but not in a boring way. The knotted napkins in a pleated fabric, and the small, round pools of candlelight, provide the essential curves that prevent the table from looking too rigid. They add a softer, more welcoming touch yet are still in keeping with the stylized, graphic approach.

LEFT: *The rectangles and squares of the storage jars, glass vases and plates make a sharp contrast to the softly knotted napkins.*
BELOW: *This sixties' inspired setting in chrome, black, and white, with a splash of red, makes for a refreshingly modern table.*

*T*HE INSPIRATION FOR THIS TABLE came from the antique blue and white soup tureen which is filled with hyacinths and ranunculi. Although the china looks coordinated, nothing on this traditional table is part of a set. All the blue and white pieces are different, but this doesn't matter. In fact, it adds to the success of the look as it is not so obvious. The table is really a collection of things that could have been passed down by your grandmother. First, there is the

ABOVE: *These antique soda siphons are beautiful to look at and their color adds an accent to the table.*
RIGHT: *Mismatched blue and white china looks great on the table.*
FAR RIGHT: *The tureen filled with flowers is the focus of the table.*

crisp white damask tablecloth and heavy napkins – very traditional. The napkins are tied with conventional antique silver napkin rings. A pair of pewter altar candlesticks stands in the center of the table topped with tall church candles, and willow pattern plates sit at each place setting. Just so that the whole table didn't become too predictably old-fashioned, I added the painted tortoiseshell tin plates to provide an unexpected and modern touch.

Although the two blue antique soda siphons no longer work, they are nevertheless very decorative, adding a flash of a sharper blue that enlivens the blue and white scheme.

FAR LEFT: *Mismatched blue and white china blends perfectly, creating a traditional table with some unexpected modern touches.*
LEFT: *Sparkling antique glassware adds a shimmering touch.*

T HE STARTING POINT for this stylish, yet simple, setting was the very practical table. It folds in or out into two perfect squares. Keeping the theme of squares, I selected four terra-cotta floor tiles to act as place mats and continued the terra-cotta theme by using garden pots for the flowers, candles, and salt and pepper.

Here, I chose orange as an accent color, but any other strong color would work equally well. The napkins contrast deliberately with the terra-cotta and match the orange of the

FAR RIGHT: *The thoroughly modern textures of terra-cotta tiles and sandblasted glass add up to a minimalist look for this white table setting.*
RIGHT: *White, sandblasted glass provides the table with a stylishly contemporary look.*

daisies. The strong clean lines of the sandblasted bowls and plates and the brushed stainless steel cutlery look modern and stark, yet subtle at the same time.

The fruit in the bowls adds a decorative touch, whereas the gentle curves of the chairs add contrast to the square shapes on the table.

LEFT: *The fruit in the bowls was chosen for its decorative qualities and helps to offset the starkness of the table.*
RIGHT: *Tall white and orange daisies are tied with a length of garden string.*
BELOW: *Miniature terra-cotta flower pots provide the perfect containers for salt and pepper.*

*T*HE ORNATE PUGINESQUE CHAIRS and the solid wooden table suggested a deep dark color scheme for this grand meal. I set a black runner lengthways down the center of the table and decided to accent it with the color rust for flowers and ribbons. Because the furnishings of this room are an eclectic mixture of old and new, I chose a collection of dark objects to decorate the center of the table, each one picked because of its particularly good shape or because it worked with the color scheme.

A wonderful pair of ebony candlesticks and an armful of rust-colored rose heads piled into the upturned lid of a Chinese

FAR RIGHT: A dark and rich color scheme of black and rust seemed appropriate for this eclectic setting of old and new furniture.
RIGHT: An armful of rust-colored rose heads are piled into the lid of a Chinese "Kung" box to make a stunning centerpiece.

"Kung" box lacquered on Chinese elm complete the center-piece. The marbled plates in a rusty-orange with gold are striking against the black. I folded the black napkins first and threaded rust-colored petersham (grosgrain) ribbon between the folds. If you look closely at the napkins, you can see they are tied with two ribbons: one black and one rust. The ribbons are first tied around the napkin and then looped over each other and threaded through. Even though the setting is imposing, placing the cutlery casually on the plates made the table feel less formal.

There is something slightly oriental about rust and black with accents of orange and gold, although there was nothing eastern about the dining room. The bronze bowl filled with rose petals is a wonderful, decorative touch. I simply broke off some of the rose petals and piled them into the bowl to add a glamorous element to the table. If you fill the bowl with cool water, it can be passed around as a delicately-scented finger bowl.

LEFT: *A striking bronze bowl filled with scented rose petals brings a touch of glamor to the table.*

LEFT: *The napkins are tied with two petersham (grosgrain) ribbons: one black and one rust. The ribbons are tied around the napkins and then threaded through.*

THIS TABLE WAS DEVISED for a catered dinner party for ten guests. It was a formal occasion; family meals in this household would probably take place round the kitchen table downstairs. The atmosphere of the dining room is cool, calm and relatively dark, with a long rectangular table. The starting point was a color scheme, in this case white and gold, to lift and lighten the moss green of the walls and chairs. There was a wonderful collection of silver cutlery and a damask tablecloth that had been specially made to match the seat cushions, so I worked with these in mind.

As always, I create lines starting from the center of the table. Here, I placed a row of small glasses filled with white ranunculi in a line which stretched the length of the table meeting the existing glass candle holders.

Transparent platters edged with gold were chosen to reflect the white flowers and the green of the room. Platters, or service plates, stay on the table throughout the meal, and each course is served on a plate that sits on the platter. The effect of a see-through plate is much subtler than an opaque plate, allowing a view of the tablecloth beneath and giving the table a shimmer.

With the plates in place I wove ivy either side of the ranunculi and in horizontal lines across the table. The glasses and cutlery were placed in the trails of ivy, so the ivy appears to be growing around them. Flowers and foliage must be fresh and I had plenty of extra ivy on stand-by. Leaves placed directly on the table probably need a spray of water at the last minute.

RIGHT: *White flowers, candlelight, transparent gold-rimmed plates and trailing ivy add up to a delightful, romantic setting.*

GREEN AND WHITE ELEGANCE

Gold Fortuny-style pleated napkins are a dramatic finishing touch. I always buy a set of twelve when it comes to napkins, as they are one of the best ways of transforming a table. I knew there would be a lot of smokers at this dinner, so scented candles were vital to help disperse the smoke. These came in small fogged glass containers and were scented with tuberose, one for each place setting.

Dressing a table is like dressing yourself, a different sweater or scarf with the same suit can alter the look completely. You can create an instant new fantasy with a change of plates, glasses, napkins, cloths or cutlery.

LEFT: *Flowers must be fresh and picked to work with the overall color scheme. Cutting down the stems and placing them in small containers not only looks pretty, it means the guests can see each other across the table.*

BELOW: *The transparency of the plates and the unusual chunky glass goblets add a shimmering, almost Pre-Raphaelite feeling to the dream-like setting.*

RIGHT: *First impressions are the most important. The trailing greenery, white and gold setting, the delicate transparent plates and the trailing ivy all tell the story. Practical factors take over later when the platters will be covered with more traditional china.*

THIS RELAXED LUNCH PARTY was set up in the kitchen of a Victorian house. The pigskin chairs and the sturdy table made from old, rough hewn timber suggested to me a Mexican theme with a riot of rich colors, visual wit and all kinds of juxtaposed textures. Pewter, glass, rough wood and metal all have a part to play here and the brilliant contrasting colors such as turquoise mixed with orange, green and red, help to set the scene.

The flowers smartly lined up along the table are pepper plants housed in baked bean cans (with the labels soaked off). Tomato purée cans have been given the same treatment and contain small candles positioned at each place setting. Bromeliads and cacti also help to provide the right atmosphere and add to the exotic flavor of the theme.

As I love the effect of stripes, I chose a banner in bright green to set along the center of the table and overhang at the ends. As well as adding a dramatic band of color to the setting, the fabric pulls together the different styles of tableware. The leaf patterned plates and the variously shaped green glasses and bowls were deliberately chosen to give a random feel. Apart from adding to the theme, this is a practical solution to entertaining – when you don't have enough matching crockery, simply mix together a variety of colors and shapes.

This setting also demonstrates that you don't need a formal dining room in order to get into a party mood. Here, kitchen knives and forks sit haphazardly on the plates, adding to the

RIGHT: *A joyful riot of clashing colors: here, checkered napkins, green glass, and exotic plants bring a Mexican atmosphere to a suburban kitchen.*

MEXICAN LUNCH

informal atmosphere. The primary red flowers pick up the color of the cushions on the wooden bench, while brightly woven napkins accentuate all the colors used on the table.

Rather than buying napkins, for this look you could cut some squares of a coarsely woven fabric, then remove threads parallel to the edges to make the self-fringe. (If you'll be washing them a lot, stitch along the inner edge of the fringe to reinforce it.) The runner could be fringed in the same way if you wish.

LEFT: *Tin cans used as vases along with functional metal plates demonstrate that expense is not an essential element of style.*
BELOW: *Sometimes just a set of striking napkins can transform the table. Here, brilliantly woven checks with knotted and fringed edges help to turn a Victorian kitchen into a Mexican hacienda.*

LEFT: *The checkered theme of the napkins is echoed by the comfortable and informal range of pillows used on the chairs.*

*T*HIS ELEGANT TABLE was set in an old library where the walls were lined with rare books, giving me the idea of using books as a theme. The tablecloth was a heavily-embroidered Indian cotton, the colors of the embroidery threads providing the inspiration for the rich tones of glass and crockery. Even on this oval table, I put a scrim runner down the center to give a panel for decoration. The next step was to buy some old (but not valuable) books which I hollowed out using a craft knife, a section at a time, and

RIGHT: *A central runner works just as well on an oval table.*
BELOW: *Dark red Nicole roses fill a hollowed out book as a floral decoration for a literary supper.*

filled with dark red roses. A few small tomes from the library's shelves provide focal points on the runner, along with simple candlesticks and thick church candles.

I chose celadon green bowls, partnered with verdigris metal plates that I often use instead of place mats. The subtle green of the china was the perfect foil for the rich red glasses and first course plates, the colors echoing the embroidery on the cloth.

To accompany the white napkins, I bought old legal documents written on parchment from an antique store. Instead of using originals, you could photocopy an old document and stain the copies with tea, to look like parchment. I rolled the documents around the napkins and closed them with sealing wax.

BELOW LEFT: Old legal documents found in an antique store are rolled around the napkins and sealed with wax.
BELOW RIGHT: As this supper was in the library, I used some of the books as accessories.

RIGHT: The colors of the embroidered Indian tablecloth were the inspiration for the choice of crockery, glasses, and flowers.

BREAKFAST & TEA

*W*HAT DOES THE WORD "brunch" mean to you? I think of blue and white gingham, the Sunday newspapers, and lovely fresh bread – anything from baguettes to bagels – spread with real butter and lashings of thick jam. So, for a Sunday brunch table, I thought it would be fun to use these elements – jam jars and newspapers – as part of the table setting.

I gathered together a collection of jam jars in different shapes and sizes, and the florist provided me with the types of flowers you would find growing wild. I put a selection of different flowers in each jar, without any attempt to "arrange" them formally, and set them randomly along the table on top of the blue and white gingham runner.

My next challenge was to dream up a way to incorporate the newspaper into the theme. After toying with the idea of using it as a tablecloth, I decided to wrap the cutlery in it (although I did wrap the cutlery first in a layer of tissue paper so that it wouldn't get covered in newsprint). Of course, I also provided the guests with all the Sunday newspapers, intact – and wrapped them together with the widest navy petersham (grosgrain) ribbon I could find.

The boiled eggs are housed in shot glasses and lined up like a row of soldiers along another strip of navy ribbon. Other additions to the brunch table include the brown paper bags for the bread and croissants. These were meant to look as if I'd just been shopping in one of those wonderful New York delis and had

RIGHT: *This cheerful brunch table comes complete with the Sunday newspapers and a neat row of boiled eggs standing at attention in glass egg cups or shot glasses.*

brought the freshly-baked bread straight back to the table. An alternative to brown bags would be two or three wicker baskets. Line them with gingham napkins, then wrap these around the heated croissants to keep them warm.

My mother always instructed me never to put milk bottles or jam jars on the table without decanting them. Despite this, somehow I think it works on this table. Remember that the finishing touches are what make all the difference, and it's fun to add some wit to a table setting. If you think of all the ingredients of a theme and invent a new way of using them, it can cost you next to nothing.

ABOVE: *Cutlery wrapped individually in newspaper is an inexpensive, yet effective, idea.*
FAR LEFT: *Flowers, which almost look hand-picked straight from the garden, are bunched into simple jam jars.*
LEFT: *Striped mugs are set haphazardly on the gingham cloth, adding to the informality of this spontaneous brunch.*

*T*HIS BIEDERMEIER TABLE AND CHAIRS suggested the perfect setting for a proper old-fashioned tea – the sort I remember having at my grandmother's house. This is a traditional Victorian tea complete with bone china and silver, a tiered cake plate laden with goodies such as toasted teacakes or scones, strawberry jam with thick cream, and piping hot Indian tea served from a bone china teapot. Tea served at a table like this really is different. The smell of toasted teacakes and the taste of tea sipped from delicate bone china all add up to a special experience.

ABOVE: *The bone china teapot is wrapped with a piece of rough white linen, casually knotted on the side.*
RIGHT AND FAR RIGHT: *A traditional Victorian tea complete with scones, jam, and Indian tea.*

I started with my favorite runners, this time quite narrow strips of crisp white damask, and then added a stripe of ivory-colored petersham (grosgrain) ribbon down the center of the strip. The same ivory ribbons criss-cross the napkins, which are held by traditional, heavy silver napkin rings.

When tying the napkins in the petersham (grosgrain) ribbons, I tend to rely on trial and error, starting with one, folding the ribbons this way and that, and then copying the formula I like at each place setting. I added a couple more ribbons to the cake plate, looping them through the handle at the top.

BELOW: *A silver soup tureen filled with roses adds an elegant touch to this relaxed tea party.*

The white theme makes the whole table look fresh and inviting, and the ivory color combined with it makes it more sophisticated and less predictable. As part of this color scheme, the central silver tureen was filled with creamy-white Leonardis roses.

In an unusual and modern take on a tea cozy, I wrapped the china teapot in a piece of rough white linen which I tied in a knot to keep it in place. Although at first glance this table looks really quite traditional, it is these modern elements and unexpected touches that make the difference.

ABOVE: *Simple damask napkins look elegant with contrasting ribbons wrapped around them.*
LEFT: *White and bone-colored ribbons tied together and added to the three-tiered cake plate support the genteel theme.*

A HUGE CIRCLE OF FRUITWOOD with removable leaves, this remarkable table was an inspiration in itself. Taking the Easter theme, I placed four calico (muslin) runners in a large cross over the center of the table. The yellow daffodils, buttercups, and primroses seemed the obvious Easter color, and I brought this out in the petersham (grosgrain) ribbon that runs in a strip down the middle of each calico runner and is also wound around the napkins. This gives a rather ecclesiastical feel.

I like to play with traditional ideas yet not feel bound by them. Here, the centerpiece of the meal is an eye-catching nest of eggs. Traditionally, these might have been hard-boiled and hand-painted, or even chocolate. I decided to choose another route and present them as if newly laid, adding to the fresh country feeling. The authentic-looking nest, which looks as if it had been found in the branches of a tree, can be made simply by winding twigs around and tying them with raffia. I selected a combination of hens' and quails' eggs for the nest and placed some at random down the runners.

The rest of the decoration is entirely conventional and is exactly what you would expect to find in a country manor dining room – good silver cutlery and napkin rings, a collection of silver ornaments and simple creamy-white bone china. I couldn't resist turning the napkin rings into egg cups and then giving the napkins my petersham (grosgrain) ribbon treatment. For this I used a narrow ivory ribbon as well as the wide yellow one – the effect is therefore more interesting and elegant. Ornate

RIGHT: *I like to take my inspiration from traditional themes – in this case, an Easter tea – yet not be bound by convention.*
BELOW: *The crystal coffee sugar sticks placed on each cup fit well with the color scheme.*

RIGHT: *Ornate rose-appliquéd doilies serve as underplates and add to the Easter atmosphere.*
BELOW: *Matching my favorite runners with the Easter theme, I placed them in a large cross over the center of the table.*

rose-appliquéd linen doilies serve as underplates and add to the Easter atmosphere. The coffee sugar sticks placed onto each cup are just there for their aesthetic value – they look festive and are in keeping with the overall theme.

Part of the charm of this table is the traditional country manor setting, with the dining room chairs, the cream carpet with its square design and the golden wood table all having a part to play. I think it's important to work with items that you've already got to hand and here I chose traditional objects such as the silver cutlery, antique lace and white bone china to emphasize the character of the room.

BELOW: *This nest looks authentic and the eggs are presented as if freshly laid.*

$\mathcal{S}$PECIAL
$\mathcal{O}$CCASIONS

*A*T CHRISTMAS I LIKE TO CREATE a table which is traditional yet not too old-fashioned. Here, the scene is opulent; the table groaning with beautiful objects and awash with rich, shimmering color.

The first stage was to lay a strip of scrim the length of the table and cover it with an abundance of Christmas decorations. The unusual holly spheres were made by covering balls of florists' foam with holly leaves, pinned into position so that the pins leave

RIGHT: *A sparkling, shining table; a cornucopia of all things good.*
BELOW: *Christmas tree ornaments, an abundance of holly, antique glass, nuts, and fruit all add to the festive atmosphere.*

FAR LEFT: *Shimmering glassware surrounded by the richness of Christmas decorations creates an opulent look.*

LEFT: *Simply knotted organza napkins are embellished with a sprig of festive holly.*

silver dots all over the balls. Added to this are Indian Christmas tree ornaments in red and silver and shiny red apples polished to perfection. This household boasts a magnificent collection of Victorian cranberry-colored glass which I placed on the table, filling spare glasses to overflowing with walnuts and hazelnuts.

The color scheme took its cue from the holly and its berries. The strong colors of red and green were augmented with silver

candlesticks entwined with holly, gold filigree-patterned plates, silver underplates (used instead of place mats) and silver cutlery, creating a truly shimmering effect. Tiny silver dishes were used for salt and pepper and as small candleholders so that the room was bathed in a warm red glow.

The napkins for this Christmas table combined gold and silver in cobwebby shot organza, knotted and then finished off with a small sprig of holly tucked into them. The occasional tall glass and the stately candelabra lift the scale of the table so that the opulent effect does not look too cluttered. Everything shimmers and glows, creating a warm welcome.

LEFT: *No Christmas table would be complete without holly. Here it climbs up the antique candelabra.*
BELOW: *The red and green color scheme for this table is highlighted with plenty of gold and silver; traditional silver cutlery, gold-rimmed bone china, gold and silver napkins, and gold and silver ornaments as the finishing touch.*

*T*HIS WAS A WHIMSICAL TABLE and conceived to demonstrate that it is possible to whip up a decorative setting without too much expense and effort. Given that it was the Fourth of July, the obvious theme is the American flag with its instantly recognizable red, white and blue stars and stripes. The kitchen table setting is deliberately utilitarian, with kitchen glassware, paper napkins, paper plates and tin accessories. The mailbox holds the muffins, the tin buckets filled with sand contain myriad candles, and the tin table-sized barbecues suggest an outdoor summer supper.

The tablecloth is made of calico (muslin), painted using stencils in the style of the American flag on a huge scale. The paper plates

BELOW: The simple jugs are decorated with painted stars.

FAR RIGHT: Festive in red, white and blue, a table is transformed for a Fourth of July feast.
RIGHT: *The miniature chocolate bars look great piled into a star-shaped dish.*

are also printed with stars and stripes. Piles of paper napkins in red, white, and blue are wrapped with a petersham (grosgrain) ribbon of another color to support the color scheme.

Even if your time is limited, you can still create amusing effects for a fun occasion like this. Here, the plates have stars and stripes, but the theme would also work with red and blue plates. You might be able to find paper plates that tie in with the theme or use white plates with stars stuck onto them. The tin accessories add to the "picnic" feel of the table and have an attractive homemade quality.

The menu should feature traditional touches along with the chocolate bars and muffins. Hamburgers are the obvious choice to grill on the barbecues, followed by tubs of ice cream, chocolate chip-cookies, and so on.

RIGHT: *Tin buckets filled with sand make the perfect containers for lots of candles which, when lit, will resemble sparkling fireworks.*
BELOW: *Muffins tumble out of a traditional mailbox.*

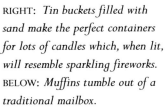

RIGHT: *Paper plates stenciled with stars and stripes make an amusing and inexpensive visual effect.*
BELOW: *Tin accessories, like these tabletop barbecues, add to the outdoor, "picnic" feel.*

$\mathcal{A}$ TABLE SET FOR HALLOWEEN has to be a nighttime table, needing the mysterious glow of the candlelit pumpkin lamps to set the mood. Think of witches, pumpkins, black magic and late October evenings and the colors of orange and black come to mind. To set the color scheme for the evening, I covered the chairs in black fabric and pinned two strips of orange petersham (grosgrain) ribbon vertically down the back. I also used a piece of scrim or upholstery linen to form a runner down the center of the table, continuing the use of strong lines.

The miniature pumpkins are used here instead of flowers. The pumpkins were deliberately chosen in varying sizes to avoid complete symmetry. The simple letterbox shape is far quicker to cut than a traditional face and, once lit with candles or little night-lights, is equally effective. Carrying the black and orange theme still further, two napkins, one of each color, were laid at each place setting, with the black napkin wrapped around the orange one. I tied the ribbon around the tops of the stems of the standard red and white wine glasses and then twirled the ribbons around the glasses.

Apart from this, the table is quite bare, ready for a menu which offers either pumpkin soup or pumpkin pie as one of the courses, not least because the pinkish-orange flesh of the pumpkin will look good against the austerity of the matte black plates. The orange-handled cutlery, laid in a dramatic cross to ward off evil, provides the final touch.

RIGHT: *A moody, magical table setting with a theme of orange and black, carried through to the ribbons, candlelit pumpkins and black crockery.*

The textures used on this table — linen, scrim, and basic petersham (grosgrain) ribbon — are all quite sober and matte, whereas the color orange, always associated with Halloween, signifies danger and demands immediate attention. The flickering glow of the candlelight and the curling of the ribbons, imitating the dancing flames of a witch's bonfire, add to the mysterious atmosphere.

RIGHT: *Orange-handled cutlery, set in a protective cross, adds to the spooky mood of the occasion.*

To give the table a more exotic look, I tied lengths of black and orange petersham (grosgrain) ribbons together and, at the last minute, twirled the wine glasses around so that the ribbons curled around the stems. These ribbons are an extremely easy way to add a festive touch to the table without any great expense or effort. Everything else is placed very simply on the table, giving a spontaneous feel to the meal.

LEFT: *Twirling petersham (grosgrain) ribbons in orange and black, twisted and curled around the stems of the glasses, add a decorative touch.*

HIS PRETTY CHRISTENING table calls for soft, pastel colors. On a cream silk tablecloth, I laid scrim runners horizontally and then added strips of wide pink petersham (grosgrain) ribbon, providing a bank of cream silk, striped scrim and pink ribbon at both ends of the buffet table. A cluster of church candles stands in the center of the table, looped back and forth with more pink ribbon. A pile of plates in alternate layers of silver and white porcelain is stacked and threaded with pink ribbon.

RIGHT: *A delicate and feminine table, with rows of champagne glasses to toast the new infant.*
BELOW: *Rosebuds, ivy and pink ribbon decorate the stack of plates.*

The final touches are lengths of trailing ivy with tiny yellow and pink rose petals scattered around the table and plates. Sugar-coated almonds are traditionally used but here, just for a change, I sprayed pebbles with silver paint.

It's a good idea to think of a way to present the cutlery that is appropriate to not only the occasion and the menu but also ties in with the theme of the presentation. Here, because this is a buffet, each set of cutlery is tied with the same pink ribbon that has been used throughout the table scheme.

LEFT: *A silver cake plate holds the sugared fruit, with roses added here and there for decoration.*
BELOW: *Knives and forks are tied together in pairs with pink ribbon; a practical as well as a pretty finishing touch.*

LEFT: *The christening table is a glistening picture of pink ribbon, trailing ivy, cream church candles, and gilt-rimmed glass. Champagne is chilling in a silver ice bucket, ready to toast the health of the new arrival.*

T HIS UNUSUAL TABLE has been designed with an attractive built-in black slate centerpiece, practical for hot dishes and usefully placed for table decoration. For this St Patrick's Day celebration, obvious themes were the color green and the shamrock. Slightly tongue-in-cheek (or with a touch of Irish blarney), I cut the leaves of a rubber plant to make a large shamrock for each place setting. Another idea was to include something to do with horses, so I added a miniature box hedge jump to the center of the table.

The room has a certain old-fashioned country feel, so fabrics like linen and wicker (for the place mats) seemed apt, as well as my

FAR RIGHT: *The built-in black slate panel running down the center of this table provides the perfect surface for hot dishes and is the starting point for decoration.*
RIGHT: *A miniature box hedge in the center of the table adds to the horsey, Irish theme.*

THE LUCK OF THE IRISH

favorite petersham (grosgrain) ribbon, used here in bottle green and cream. The crockery is edged in green and features an aristocratic crest. This is the sort of crockery you can find in antique stores. Although you'd hardly guess, the underplates with their green rims are very modern.

It's often the simple touches that inspire an idea or that coordinate the table. Here, the glass apples, as well as being the perfect shade of shamrock green, are simple but elegant. Resting on an antique crested cake plate that was part of the household crockery, they add the finishing touch.

I added green glasses to each place setting too, and some hand-blown glass candlesticks to give an added sparkle. These contrast well with the texture of the linen napkins wrapped with wide bottle-green petersham (grosgrain) ribbon and decorated with the "shamrocks."

FAR LEFT: *The glass apples are the perfect shade of shamrock green. The cake plate formed part of the crested family crockery.*
LEFT: *A shamrock, cut from a rubber plant leaf, alludes to the Irish theme and adds an amusing finishing touch.*

*W*ITH HEARTS AS THE OBVIOUS starting point for a romantic Valentine table, I just had to use this brightly colored, heart-shaped china. These plates, in a mixture of sizes and colors, look almost edible when layered red on pink and pink on blue on this amazing cobalt blue table.

The pink netting wrapped around the romantic bowl of red parrot tulips was rescued from a little girl's dressing-up box and the heart-shaped candies, sending their special messages spilling out of the champagne flutes, are children's favorites. Candles in marshmallow-pink set on heart-shaped candleholders and heart-shaped dishes of sweets continue the theme.

Three different types of glasses hold champagne, champagne, and yet more champagne. All three are decorated with gold, while the baroque strawberry and gilt tumblers, which look rather like Moroccan tea glasses, have gold hearts painted on the sides. Extra candles (can there ever be too many?) are set in tiny, brightly-colored pots rimmed with gold. The decorative cutlery includes heart-shaped spoons and an ornateness that would melt the hardest of hearts.

With the hand-painted marbled table, the china and flamboyant cutlery, this dinner à deux bordered on the kitsch. I, therefore, decided to emphasize the theme by adding pleated napkins and napkin rings resembling the huge, unsubtle rings that pop out of Christmas crackers. They are the perfect kitsch finishing touch for this table, just in case HE forgets to bring one with him!

RIGHT: *A fine romance; a table with a heart-shaped theme and somewhat kitsch overtones.*
BELOW: *Heartbreaking clashes of colors and textures — sugar pink net sits alongside dark red, velvety tulips, painted glass, and multicolored cutlery.*

Sugar-pink and romantic ruby-red are the main colors for any Valentine table. Here, the table has a frothy, feminine flavor.

A less tongue-in-cheek setting could be created by using pale pink fabrics with contrasting red tones. You could even paint or stencil gold hearts onto the tablecloth and napkins to continue the theme.

FAR LEFT: *Heart-shaped plates in romantic colors are layered one on top of the other.*
ABOVE: *Napkins are secured with an oversized "jeweled" ring.*
LEFT: *Light-hearted and colorful, the pink paper napkins are wrapped around the cutlery and tied with gold ribbon.*

THEME PARTIES

*W*HEN I ASKED MY HUSBAND how he'd like to celebrate his birthday, he asked for an Indian take-out meal surrounded by his closest friends. It was a little more elaborate than he'd expected. But essentially I staged the whole meal on a large Indian coffee table measuring about 3 x 2 metres (10 x 6 feet). Because the table is very low, we all sat around on big calico cushions.

The decor of the whole room provided the "Indian" setting, with a decorative mixture of antique paisleys, Madras striped sofa cushions, rattan blinds and an exotic leopard print thrown into the mix because its brown and orangey tones worked with the deep paprika and chilli reds of the rest of the decor.

Because the table was low, the flowers also had to be low. I floated heads of sunflowers and marigolds, chosen for their color, in water-filled, brass bowls. Dozens of tiny terra-cotta-based nightlights were grouped on Indian brass plates, so the whole table glowed in the dark. Stone plates and wrought iron cutlery, set on the old wood table with a generous sprinkling of dried chillis over it, added to the ethnic atmosphere.

The color scheme was inspired by oriental spices – cumin, coriander and cinnamon – plus the deeper reds of fabrics from Rajastan. The napkins were paper ones that I found which just happened to be decorated with chillis. I tied them up in knotted rope. Because one tends to drink beer with curry, I put large, green glass tumblers at every place setting and didn't bother with glasses for wine.

BELOW: *Calico cushions form the main seating for this informal dinner while a pile of patterned and Indian paisley cushions add an atmospheric touch.*

OVERLEAF AND RIGHT: *An ethnic feast set on an old wooden table where people can sit around on cushions while the candles glow throughout.*
BELOW: *Utilitarian stone plates make the perfect choice to serve curry and rice. The green glasses are a generous size for beer while the paper napkins tied in rope are both practical and decorative.*

THIS ELEGANT AND STYLISH TABLE setting looks sophisticated and rather special, but it came about because I invited some friends round to celebrate a birthday, and I didn't have time to cook. What I have created here is a setting for a take-out meal.

I was inspired originally by the square glass plates. To enhance their sculptural simplicity, a Japanese theme seemed ideal with a minimalist, uncluttered approach. Saki glasses, rather than wine glasses were required – they are not authentic, but modern hand-blown glasses completely in tune with the overall effect.

Japanese flower arrangements rely on texture and shape for their impact, rarely on color, and the shape and size of the container is as important as the choice of bloom or leaf. Fortunately I had time to warn the florist that I wanted some large shiny leaves – water lily leaves would have been ideal – to decorate the table. I also arranged some white guelder roses with spiky grasses inside three Japanese baskets to create the centerpiece. Smooth river-washed stones and moss from the garden gave the table a calm, zen-like feeling, and clusters of tiny eight-hour night light candles on stone platters burned throughout the meal.

For real authenticity, it should have been black on black, but the Black Watch tartan tablecloth was all I had, and I liked the way the subtle check echoed the shape of the plates and the green of the foliage. Huge platters of sushi and black table napkins, ringed with rope napkin holders which conveniently doubled as a rest for the chopsticks, completed the picture.

BELOW: *Black napkins tied with knotted rope add a twist of Japanese minimalism.*

RIGHT AND BELOW: *This table setting combines all the textures and shapes of a Japanese garden with large shiny leaves, spiky grasses, smooth stones and tufted moss. Natural materials extend to the wooden chopsticks and the knotted rope napkin rings.*

RIGHT: *To recreate a Japanese setting, keep the table uncluttered, select china and glass with simple, clean lines, and keep to just one or two colors. Add a few authentic touches, such as the chopsticks and the Saki-style glasses.*

CHRISTMAS, A NEW YEAR'S EVE supper or simply a menu with a Scottish theme could be the occasion for a tartan table like this. It started with the idea of using large safety pins (similar to kilt pins) on the tartan napkins, instead of conventional rings. A bold runner crosses the table, blending with napkins in another red plaid. A third tartan decorates the upper plates, while the ribbons that tie the cutlery match the table runner. You could, of course, use someone's personal tartan for any of these.

Heather is the obvious choice for the floral decorations, and the small pink plants are placed in silver whiskey goblets. Simple glasses seem appropriate, and whiskey is the preferred tipple.

FAR RIGHT: *A multitude of glowing candles enhance the table at this tartan supper.*
RIGHT: *Underplates (chargers) are now the more stylish alternative to place mats. Here I have used two — a large plain green plate and one with a red border picking up the red of the tartan.*

A TARTAN TABLE

FAR RIGHT: *Stacks of plates in complementary reds and greens sit at each place setting.*
BELOW RIGHT: *Kilt pins tie up the napkins – a witty detail that is appropriate for a Highland theme.*
BELOW: *The massed candles create a dramatic yet slightly ethereal effect, glowing like fireflies.*

Having chosen red and green tartans as a starting point, it was the addition of witty or evocative details that made the idea work. The whiskey glasses holding the flowering heather, the kilt pins to tie the napkins, the candleholders with their trailing tartan ribbons, the tartan around the rim of the top plates, and the simple tartan ribbon tying the cutlery together all transformed a simple wooden table and chairs into a warm and welcoming Highland retreat.

*T*HIS TABLE WAS ACTUALLY INSPIRED by my daughter and step-daughters who maintained that I had to include a table for teenagers in this book. After a certain amount of discussion, their definition of a dream teenage table included two important ingredients: tie-dyeing and floating candles. So that was my starting point.

A circular table flanked by chairs with curvy wrought-iron backs and primary colored seats helped to set a cheerful background. The napkins were tie-dyed to match in the brightest range of primary colors and the floating flower-shaped candles glowed among dahlia heads in brilliant shades. The colors of the flowers and napkins were picked up again in a set of glasses in red, blue,

FAR LEFT: *The vases for the multicolored daisies were old ice cream cartons, the contents of which were served for supper.*
LEFT: *Candy letters made from brightly-colored jelly used as place settings add a youthful touch.*
RIGHT: *The definition of a teenage dream table included two important ingredients: tie-dyeing and floating candles.*

purple, green and yellow. Jelly letters identify the place settings and, instead of plates, I used fluted baking pans to echo the fluted edges of the candles and flower petals.

The aim of this table is to be youthful, fresh, and pretty. Bright colors are an obvious choice, and all the ingredients are inexpensive. Dahlias and daisies both come in a variety of primary colors and the familiar colors of the red, pink, yellow and orange flower heads all work together effectively. The ice cream cartons are both fun and practical and at the same time you know the contents won't go to waste.

FAR LEFT: *The floating candles, shaped like flowers, have a slightly "hippie" quality.*
LEFT: *All the ingredients used on this table are inexpensive, including the flan dishes used as unusual plates.*
ABOVE: *The tie-dyed napkins have added "flower-power."*

A CAREFREE HOLIDAY LUNCH, this table has all the earthy colors and natural textures of an African safari location. Spiky palm fronds, dried grasses, old tanned leather, rope, rattan, ethnic fabrics, sun, sand, deep dark henna reds, earth browns, and leafy greens all combine to create the right atmosphere.

The glasses were bought with string already bound around the stems, but you could easily decorate your own glasses in the same way. Lengths of authentic African fabric are thrown over the backs of the chairs to bring them into character. The ethnic bowls, plates and cutlery, now easy to find having been imported from all over Africa, sit at each place on a grass place mat.

I didn't exactly neglect my signature strips when I planned this African table, but I made a central display of exotic fruits in a strip instead. Wonderfully visual and colorful tropical fruits such as papaya, pomegranate, prickly pear, and custard apple (luckily now all available in local supermarkets) were the obvious choice and I laid them on the huge rectangular leaves of a palm tree. The spiky fruit echoes the spiky palm fronds and conjures up the idea of a seaside lunch in Africa or the Caribbean. The fruits can either form part of the meal or serve purely as decoration.

The unusual wooden cutlery is tied with string looped around the simple white napkin in a laid-back fashion. My florist found the pieces of bark that serve as bread or fruit baskets.

Having a theme allows you to be inventive and look for pieces you already own, such as dishes, bowls, or ornaments that fit in with the theme you've chosen. Anything natural – wood, raffia, rope, or stone – as opposed to manufactured and sophisticated would be suitable for the African theme. However, it is interesting that if the mix and the colors are right, you can hardly tell which pieces are authentic and which are modern. On this table, the distinctive glasses were really all I needed to bring the whole theme together. They automatically looked ethnic. The pieces of fabric were the most authentic African element: the result of world-wide traveling by the owner of this dining room.

PREVIOUS PAGES: *All the natural textures of Africa are to be found on this table: palm fronds, banana leaves, raffia, rope, carved wood, and rattan.*
LEFT: *As a centerpiece for this table, a palm leaf holds a selection of exotic fruits, including custard apples, papayas, mangoes, and pomegranates.*
BELOW: *The simple white napkins and African spoons are tied with lengths of raffia to mark each place setting.*

I<small>T'S HARD TO BELIEVE</small> that the dedicated sports fan would have time to concentrate on good food or a beautifully laid table during an important game, but for this lunch at a sports stadium, my aim was to devise a table to reflect the location and the occasion.

Flowers and foliage are the first things to consider for any table, and for this lunch it just had to be grass. Small loaf pans containing fresh green tufts of grass, rooted in soil, sit alongside each place setting. The other sporting elements that immediately

FAR RIGHT: *Materials and fabrics associated with sports are used: tweed, flannel, velvet, and horn.* RIGHT: *Horn whistles and black laces tie up the napkins: obvious sporting accessories that add an amusing touch.*

came to mind were the textures of horn, bone, and black slate, so I gathered together accessories made from them.

The rich mixture of textures that makes me think of sports includes the tailored tweeds associated with riding and hacking jackets (the type of tweed jacket worn with soft woolen trousers). For this reason, I covered the chairs with a traditional Prince of Wales check and buttoned them with brown velvet. The overall effect is very masculine, enhancing the tones of black and brown, as well as the splashes of green grass, both on the table and viewed through the window.

The cutlery is set simply and squarely, and the glass goblets suggest a fine claret will be drunk. To prevent the table setting from becoming too dark, I used black-and-white plates, which add pizazz and a modern touch.

FAR LEFT: *I always decorate a table with flowers, but on this particular occasion, small tins of grass turf seemed more appropriate to the stadium setting.*
LEFT: *The silver-rimmed horn glasses are very evocative of "hunting, shooting and fishing" and the salt and pepper with their insignias reinforce the "members only" club effect.*

*T*HIS WAS THE BOARDROOM of a successful lingerie company and, as well as having quite a feminine atmosphere for a boardroom, it had also been painted a bright and contemporary turquoise. The table and chairs (a copy of the popular fifties' Swedish design) are made from blond wood, as are the picture frames on the wall. This made it almost obligatory to play with color, although the table decoration had to be subtle to avoid distracting the participants at the meeting.

This table was an exercise in layering color. As it was for a company at the cutting edge of the fashion business, I wanted it to look contemporary. The combination of mauve, pink, lime, and yellow for the pyramid of crockery and place mats achieved that goal, especially when set against the turquoise walls.

I decided to work with a range of spring-like pastels, starting with the sheets of pale mauve construction paper which I used as the bottom layer for the pyramid of crockery. Next came a folded copy of a financial newspaper, appropriate for the boardroom setting and distinctive for its pink coloring. The top three layers were pale lime and yellow with a pale lime cup and saucer at the top.

With all those pastel shades, the flowers had to be daffodils, their bright yellow contrasting brilliantly with the turquoise walls. Since this was a sandwich lunch, I opted for triangular plastic packaging from the sandwiches and used each one to "plant" the daffodils, surrounding them with moss. I have to admit that the

RIGHT: *As this was a lunch for a company at the forefront of the fashion business, I wanted to give the table a contemporary look.*
BELOW: *A layering of strong, contemporary colors — turquoise, yellow, mauve, and pink — sets just the right mood.*

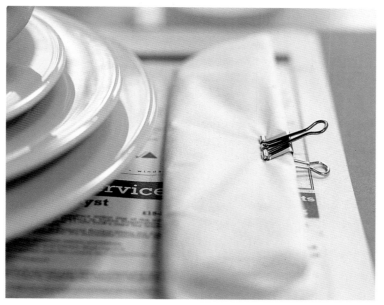

brand of mineral water was chosen entirely because of the color of the glass bottle, and the central plate of apples was another aesthetic addition (as well as an edible one). A notepad and pencil were placed next to each place setting, and the white napkins were secured with a paper fastener.

The paper fastener used to secure the napkins and the financial newspaper which is used as a place mat were, of course, very inexpensive accessories, totally in keeping with the occasion and providing amusing conversation pieces. The same applies to the sandwich containers which have been used as vases. Simple ideas which tie in with the occasion and are economical to achieve are often the best and most effective.

Thinking laterally is also important. Who are the people at lunch? What would they appreciate? There is no reason, for instance, why place mats should be made in any specific fabric, shape, or size. In this case, the thick paper folded twice was practical and absorbent as well as pretty, and can simply be thrown away after lunch.

*W*HEN I STARTED THINKING ABOUT girlfriends' lunchtime preferences, I came up with the mineral water bottle idea. After the labels were soaked off, small bottles were placed in the center of the table and filled with tulips. The tablecloth is a series of photocopies of magazine covers. The same idea could be used for photocopies of theatre programmes, sheet music or anything else that was of interest to the group.

The napkin ties were easy — just lengths of faux pearls available from department stores. I tied these around the black and white napkins and secured each rope of pearls around a lipstick — a gift for the lunchtime companions.

With the photocopies of magazines as the tablecloth, a black and white theme was inevitable. The Roman plates, each featuring a different Doric column, worked perfectly with black dessert plates, clear glass, stylish bowls and the lipstick cases. The result is very graphic, clever and, above all, fun.

PREVIOUS PAGE: *At a girlfriends' lunch, mineral water is often the most popular tipple. The mineral water bottles, used as vases, are an apt reminder.*
FAR LEFT: *A tablecloth with a difference: if conversation flags during lunch, you can always read the magazine covers!*
LEFT: *A black and white theme with stylish accessories: a magazine tablecloth, ropes of pearls, and fashionable lipsticks.*

*F*OR THIS LUNCH I put my signature strip down the center of the table but moved away from my usual choice of fabric. Here, I chose a strip of garden complete with soil and moss, heather and roses, along with herbs such as rosemary, thyme, mint, and chives.

As this table was in a garden room complete with colonial style rattan chairs, the whole feeling was light and airy: a scene that lent itself to adding even more glass. Here I used huge wine glasses, watery blue-green colored glass plates and candles in

FAR LEFT: *I couldn't resist these miniature watering cans as containers for the salt and pepper.* LEFT: *For the central panel of this table, I planted a strip of garden, complete with roses and herbs.* RIGHT: *The whole feel of the conservatory was light and airy: a scene that lent itself to adding even more glass.*

GARDEN ROOM LUNCH

glass jars positioned along the length of the window. To give the table more of a garden atmosphere, I chose wooden plates and tied the damask napkins with green wire that gardeners use to tie back plants. More candles flicker in individual beds of moss.

I always put flowers or a floral display on the table. Here, there were so many shades of green in the herbal garden in the center of the table that I felt it needed just a touch of color. These miniature roses with their delicate pink heads were just right.

ABOVE: *Wooden plates and white damask napkins tied with gardeners' green wire add to the conservatory setting.*
RIGHT: *The place settings are moss-filled terra-cotta pots with plant labels for the guests' names.*
LEFT: *I always like to put flowers or some sort of floral display on the table. Here, miniature roses are entwined in the greenery, providing a touch of color.*

*T*HE *RAISON D'ETRE* BEHIND THIS TABLE setting was to create the perfect portable picnic: a setting for an *alfresco* meal that was nothing to do with rugs, canvas stools, paper plates, and plastic cutlery. The answer was a simple trestle table that could be packed up and taken anywhere, and some classic folding teak chairs. For the table, the style was to be simple yet smart. Beautiful glasses, flowers, and china always make food taste better.

A runner works perfectly on an outdoor table because it allows a plain tablecloth to be transformed to suit the setting. This runner was made from a length of antique mattress ticking with

FAR RIGHT: *A simple white damask cloth and cream calico cushions are transformed with the navy and white runner and slip covers that set the nautical theme. The top plate, with its strong navy stripe, coordinates with the fabric. For the next course, to soften the graphic effect of the stripes, the second plate is plain white with a raised floral pattern on the rim.*
RIGHT: *Summery, cool, crisp, and clean-looking, blue and white is a totally appropriate color scheme for an outdoor setting.*

a strong navy and white stripe, but similar fabrics are readily available. Blue and white are ideal summer colors and give the table a nautical flavour. The same ticking was used for slip covers for the cushions and chair seats. Designed like half an envelope so the cream calico cushions poke out, these slip covers are easy to make and can be used to ring the changes. The damask napkins have nautical knotted rope rings to hold them in place.

Brilliant blue grape hyacinths, tucked into little galvanized metal pots with an outer ring of moss, line up smartly down the center of the table to echo the stripes of the runner. Blue and white china was a natural choice, each place setting sitting on a shiny pewter platter. Crisp navy and white petersham ribbons tied around the stems of the wine glasses added a fun finishing touch.

FAR LEFT: *In late spring, sharp blue grape hyacinths were still available, but cornflowers would make an alternative summer choice. Flowers running the full length of the table should be kept low, about the height of the tallest wine glass.*

LEFT: *Pewter platters double as place mats, matching the metal of the flowerpots. A quick and easy alternative to the knotted rope napkin rings is a length of petersham (grosgrain) ribbon wrapped around the napkins.*

DESIGN DETAILS

 LOWERS

No table would be complete without flowers. Even if they do not provide the initial inspiration for my theme, I know they will play a major, decorative part in every design, becoming the focal point of any table setting.

Tying these orange daisies with a length of simple garden string is a vital detail, making the display seem far more informal.

Delicate rose heads strewn randomly on the table add a touch of romance, elegance, and style.

A jam jar full of wild flowers placed on a gingham-covered table gives the impression that they were hand-picked from the garden.

At this informal brunch table, the floral display needs to be unsophisticated and unpretentious.

A generous antique tureen filled with pure white ranunculi and beautifully scented blue hyacinths immediately becomes the focal point for this charming blue and white table.

It's important to use wit and ingenuity when choosing vases, like these galvanized metal pots, used here as vases for an outdoor picnic.

Tulips are modern and graphic, especially in deep shades. The contrast of the red flowers with the shocking pink net is important, unexpected, and dramatic.

There's no need to be too sophisticated when planning a teenage party. This empty ice cream carton used as a vase hits the right note.

Creamy, old-fashioned roses are best displayed in simple containers, such as this stylish clear glass vase.

Sunflowers always make a dramatic effect. Here, their dark yellow petals and brown centers complement the Indian-style table.

Nothing is more beautiful than the darker-tinged edges of Nicole roses, here piled into the center of a book which has been carved out to hold the stems.

It's important to use seasonal touches on the table. Here, holly twisted around an antique silver candelabra is the obvious decoration for Christmastime.

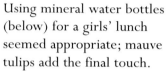

Using mineral water bottles (below) for a girls' lunch seemed appropriate; mauve tulips add the final touch.

TYING NAPKINS

I collect sets of napkins in all sorts of fabrics and colors from wherever I travel. They provide a simple way to add atmosphere and color to a table, and can be tied, knotted, or held together in any number of ways.

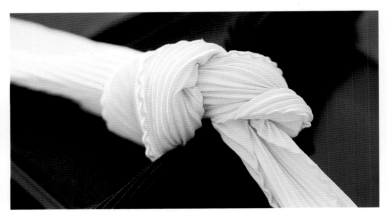

Petersham (grosgrain) ribbon comes in almost every possible width and color imaginable. Here a wide navy band wraps the Sunday newspapers, keeping them neat and tidy.

This knotted napkin in a pleated fabric brings a feminine, possibly even oriental, look to the table. The material used here is soft and pliable, allowing it to be tied in all manner of ways, and will not be too creased when unknotted.

These napkins are tied together with an inexpensive string of faux pearls and a lipstick. Feminine and fun.

Bright checks and fringes suggest a Mexican carnival atmosphere. The simple knotting of these cotton napkins adds to the casual and cheerful look of the table.

A glamorous occasion demands a glamorous fabric, like this organza. The sprig of holly adds the seasonal touch to a festive table.

Use the same "ingredients" for each place setting, but vary them by tying and embellishing each napkin differently.

A band of plaited brown leather is ideal for a lunch in the natural surroundings of a conservatory.

For adding "flower power" to a tie-dyed napkin, the dahlia is the perfect choice.

Two neat rings of rope, precisely knotted and enclosing a white damask napkin, give just the right flavor of the outdoors for an al fresco lunch.

A simple paper fastener provides a clever way to fasten a napkin for a sandwich lunch in the boardroom.

Contrasting lengths of ribbon wrapped around a traditional napkin make the whole occasion look more special.

A sporty accessory is used to tie up napkins at a sporting lunch. Think topical for occasions like this, and introduce an element of fun.

$\mathcal{P}$LACE SETTINGS

There is no reason why a place mat has to be a place mat. It could be a book, a second plate, a piece of folded paper, a magazine, or even a terra-cotta floor tile. There are no rules if you're inventive.

Here, I used a picture book as a place mat for a children's lunch, with twisted orange peel twirled round the napkins. It adds a touch of fun to the table. Choose a book with a washable cover in case of spills (or use tear sheets from a favourite comic).

This was an exercise in color and shape. A terra-cotta garden tile seemed the obvious choice, contrasting with the colors and textures of the crockery.

The appropriate choice of magazine makes a perfect place mat, and it is both heat-resistant and non-slip.

This is minimal and utilitarian in feel: brown paper on the wooden table, kitchen knives and forks, and rice cakes.

As a theme, tartan gives you plenty of color to play with. Here the underplate becomes a mat for the tartan-edged plate.

A neat pyramid of crockery in toning pastel colors starting from a lilac base. This place mat was a piece of construction paper folded in half, topped with a copy of a business newspaper.

Here I used a round, appliquéd lace doily as a place mat. It is very feminine, with an old-fashioned, country appeal. A paper doily would be equally effective.

A mixture of textures and colors take their inspiration from the old Indian crewelwork tablecloth.

Layers of color make an effective setting. The heart-shaped dishes are perfect for the food of love.

LACE NAMES

As with everything else on the table, you can be inventive with place cards. They need not be formally printed or written in script. Here are a few suggestions to get you started.

Smartly embossed initials (right), white on white, would be perfect for an elegant wedding reception or for a formal dinner.

A pile of smooth stones and a starfish support a brown paper card.

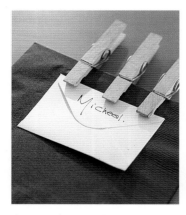

An envelope containing a hand-written message is attached with three clothes-pins to a paper napkin.

Search in your kitchen cupboards for unusual accessories which make amusing additions to a kitchen table. Here, plastic clothesline and clothes-pins make a fun idea for a casual lunch.

Write guests' names on lengths of colored ribbon and attach them to a flower in a matching color.

Playing with stripes: here, the name is written on the ribbon and a flower marks the spot.

With some imagination, all sorts of stationery items can become good place setting accessories. Here a paper fastener has been used.

A length of bamboo holds a hessian linen napkin with a neatly typed name label for a garden party.

A simple luggage label and some chopsticks neatly encased in ribbon.

Miniature plant pots can be used for place cards too.

A plain drinking glass uses sprigs of mimosa to secure a card, and a clothes-pin clips its partner in position on the edge of another glass.

TRAYS

Why should a tray be written off as being utilitarian and therefore unattractive? A decorative tray will cheer you up when you're feeling ill or be a romantic gesture for your partner. It is also perfect for light meals in the garden or can add a sense of occasion even to a meal destined to be eaten sitting on the couch.

A bandage around the napkin, a Red Cross place mat, a thermometer, and an empty pill bottle serving as flower pot should make any invalid smile.

I love this jar with its smart silver cap. It's ideal for the monochrome look of this black and white breakfast tray: the perfect way to start the day.

So delicate and ethereal, these sandblasted glasses, the clear glass plates, and the unusual, glass-handled cutlery look just right on a circular silver tray.

Take-out food cartons on a tray lined with a Chinese newspaper. The green luster china, lacquered chopsticks, and black ribbon around the napkin make it look special.

Here I was playing with color and texture with wooden plates, the wicker tray, white china, and white ceramic fruit. You just know the food will taste delicious.

There's something very French about the combination of blue and white gingham and matching china, so I wrapped the marmalade jars with a sheet of French newspaper.

ANDLES

I can't resist putting candles on the table, even in the daylight. They have practical uses too, as they prevent cigarette smoke from lingering. There is nothing prettier than flickering lights and it's also more flattering to the complexion.

Floating candles are sometimes considered a little tasteless, but here they fill the bill perfectly, bringing a youthful and charming look to the table. Instead of individual bowls, the candles could be placed in one large container.

You just have to have candles at Halloween. Spookily flickering from a pumpkin or two, they add to the magical atmosphere.

These lights glow like fireflies in the night. The whole effect would have been less ethereal with electric lights.

This is a lunch party (right) held in an airy garden room. The flickering of the candles is reflected in the windows, adding even more light to the occasion. This demonstrates that candles work just as well in daylight.

Even the simplest of nightlights placed haphazardly all around the table add to the atmosphere.

ACKNOWLEDGMENTS

I would like to thank Arabella McNie for all the time and help that
she has given to this book – thank you.
Thanks to Ricca who has been indispensable.
Special thanks to all of my clients and friends who have allowed me
into their homes to decorate their tables.

Particular thanks to the following without whose especial help the book
would have remained incomplete.
Maryse Boxer and Carolyn Quartermaine chez Joseph;
John Carter at the Flower Van; Thomas Goode; Dickens and Jones;
Jerry's Home Store

The author would also like to thank the following companies for their
generosity in loaning tableware and other props for this book.

Aero; Bentleys; Colour Blue; David Mellor; Designers Guild; The Dining
Room Shop; Fired Earth; The General Trading Company; H.V. Caldicott Ltd;
ICTC; Monogrammed Linen Shop; Muji; Mulberry Hall; Nina Campbell;
Osborne & Little; Richard Taylor Designs; The Room; Royal Worcester;
Snapdragon; The Source; Theo Fennell; Verandah; Villeroy and Boch;
The White House; William Yeoward.

INDEX